# My Guide Inside®

*Knowing Myself and Understanding My World*
*(Book I)*
*Teacher's Manual*
*For Introduction, Primary MGI Learner Book*

*Christa Campsall*
*with*
*Kathy Marshall Emerson*

*3 Principles Ed Talks*
*myguideinside.com*

© 2018 Christa Campsall  Updated 2020

www.myguideinside.com

*My Guide Inside*® is a registered trademark of Christa Campsall (3 Principles Ed Talks)
ISBN-13:  978-1981469192
ISBN-10:  1981469192
Library of Congress Control Number: 2017919711
CreateSpace Independent Publishing Platform (a subsidiary of Amazon.com)
Charleston, SC

All rights reserved.
No part of this work covered by copyrights hereon may be reproduced or used in any form or by any means—graphic, electronic or mechanical—without the prior written permission of the author, except for reviewers who may quote brief passages. Any request for photocopying, recording, taping or storage on information retrieval systems for any part of this work shall be directed in writing to the author.

First Printing, 2018
Printed in the United States of America
Authored With: Kathy Marshall Emerson
Conceptual Development: Barbara Aust and Kathy Marshall Emerson
Design: Josephine Aucoin
Production: Tom Tucker
Contributions: Dr. William Pettit, Dr. Marjorie Hawkins, Lori Smith and Barbara Aust
Webmaster: Michael Campsall

E-books, MGI Online, Video on Demand, Video Clips, and Digital Media Options:
See www.myguideinside.com for these resources.

### Why an Owl?

Over the years as a classroom teacher, Christa was given various owl gifts. She loves them as symbols of the wisdom we all share. Starting in ancient times and throughout history, various cultures have seen the owl as linked with wisdom and guidance. The owl's big, round eyes symbolize seeing knowledge. Although it is sometimes linked to other ideas, it is because of this connection to wisdom, guidance, and seeing knowledge that the owl was chosen as the graphic symbol for *My Guide Inside (MGI)*. Christa hopes this interpretation is also meaningful to you. One of her former students, Jo Aucoin, now a graphic artist, was commissioned to create the *MGI* owls and clouds graphics.

*My Guide Inside® (Book I) Teacher's Manual*

# Contents

**Promise of Change**
    Outcomes: What Primary Students Report ................................. iv
    Foreword ............................................................................................ v
    Objectives of *My Guide Inside* ...................................................... vi
    Encouragement to Teachers ............................................................ 1

**Overview for Teaching *My Guide Inside*** ........................................ 2
**Sharing the Principles in Early Childhood Programs** ................... 7
**Key Teaching Points for Lessons** ....................................................... 8
**Introduction to Objectives and Lesson Plans** ................................. 9
    <u>Learning the Foundation</u>
    Lesson Plan Chapter 1 Discovering My Guide Inside ................... 10
    Lesson Plan Chapter 2 My Feelings Come from Thought ........... 12
    <u>Learning from Life</u>
    Lesson Plan Chapter 3 Happiness Inside Me ................................ 14
    Lesson Plan Chapter 4 Fast and Furious or Calm and Curious ... 16
    Lesson Plan Chapter 5 Enjoying Friendship ................................. 18
    Lesson Plan Chapter 6 Being A-okay Today ................................. 20
    <u>Moving Forward</u>
    Lesson Plan Chapter 7 Seeing and Helping Others ...................... 22
    Lesson Plan Chapter 8 Knowing Myself ....................................... 24
    Lesson Plan Chapter 9 Dandy Words ............................................ 28

**Assessment and Observation** ............................................................ 29
**Integrating *My Guide Inside* in Education** ................................... 34
    Current Education Policy Context ................................................ 34
    Educational Learning Objectives and Competencies ................. 36
**Supplemental Resources** .................................................................. 38
    Recommended Three Principles Resources ................................ 38
    Continued Learning for Educators ............................................... 38
    Websites ........................................................................................... 40
    Instructional Materials for Learners .............................................. 40
***My Guide Inside* in Context of Current Research and Theory** ... 41
**Acknowledgments** ............................................................................. 45
**Overview of My Guide Inside Comprehensive Curriculum** ........ 46
    About the Authors ......................................................................... 46
    What Professionals Say About *My Guide Inside* ........................ 48

*My Guide Inside® (Book 1) Teacher's Manual*

## *Outcomes: What Primary Students Report*

*Real students, aged 5-7, whom we have been privileged to work with, describe their experiences learning the principles that My Guide Inside (MGI) explores:*

✠ "Wisdom whispers to me."

✠ "The best thing I learned from my guide inside solved all my problems. And my problem was I worried too much."

✠ "I learned to listen to my little voice inside."

✠ "I learned that everyone has a guide inside them. If you use it you will do the right choice."

✠ "I have learned to not get involved in conflict."

✠ "Being a good friend even if we disagree."

✠ "The best thing I learned was stay calm and curious instead of fast and furious."

✠ "The best thing I learned was holding onto bad [thoughts] is not good."

✠ "The best thing I learned was to get rid of bad [thoughts]. I let them go."

✠ "That the sun behind that bad cloud is always shining."

✠ "I can control myself and be less distracted."

✠ "I trust what I think and feel good about it. I am feeling more brave. You have to trust and be brave."

✠ "The best thing I learned was being a-okay is natural."

*My Guide Inside® (Book 1) Teacher's Manual*

# *Foreword*

 If you are reading this book, you and your students are beginning an extraordinary life-changing process. I am a psychiatrist old enough to be the grandfather of your students. I would like to share a very personal message with you.

I had to stumble and bumble doing the best I could with limited understanding of my true nature. I did not know how my moment-to-moment experience was created. I had no clue wisdom was available to guide me through all the challenges in my life.

I spent 26 years in school to become a psychiatrist, but I did not learn about true mental health. For many years while I was treating patients I was personally depressed.

I got lucky! I had the opportunity to learn the Three Principles and my life and clinical practice changed forever. Trust me, having the three universal principles of Mind, Thought and Consciousness shared with your students, which is the purpose of *My Guide Inside*, is the most precious and life changing gift possible!

These universal principles will introduce your students to their true nature and the inside-out nature of experience. *My Guide Inside* points students to the ever-present internal guidance of wisdom. For the rest of their lives whenever they are faced with challenges and uncertainties these lessons will be PRICELESS!

When I was six and my brother was three, he took his hands off the glass Coca Cola bottle and grabbed the straw in the bottle. He watched with surprise, dismay and confusion as the bottle and its contents went crashing and splashing to the floor. I have never forgotten the principle of gravity.

I share this, as a man, who traversed growing up himself; as a father, who helped raise four children; and as a psychiatrist with more than 40 years of experience and Board Certification in Adolescent Psychiatry, who assisted young clients in their journey to adulthood. I have dreamed of a day when young children would have the learning opportunity you are providing.

Understanding principles of mental health makes a difference, too!!! Thank you for guiding your students on the journey to happiness!

*Dr. William (Bill) Pettit*
*Psychiatrist*

*My Guide Inside® (Book 1) Teacher's Manual*

# Objectives of My Guide Inside

The principles Dr. Pettit refers to operate in all people, including every child. This *MGI* curriculum points the way to wholeness, happiness, creativity and well-being in all parts of every student's life.

Therefore, *MGI* has these two academic goals for students:
**(1)** Enhance Personal Well-being with an understanding of these principles, and
**(2)** Develop competencies in Communication, Thinking, and Personal and Social Awareness and Responsibility.
*MGI* accomplishes both goals by using stories, discussion and various written and creative activities, as the learning increases your students' competency in English Language Arts.

Discovering their guide inside is key to learning and enhances students' ability to make decisions, navigate life and build healthy relationships. Accessing natural wisdom will affect their well-being, spiritual wellness, personal and social responsibility, and positive personal and cultural identity. Social emotional learning, including self-determination, self-regulation and self-efficacy, are also natural outcomes of greater awareness.

*My Guide Inside® (Book I) Teacher's Manual*

# Encouragement to Teachers

Welcome to a wonderful new experience sharing the principles Dr. Pettit talks about, commonly called Three Principles, with your students. I have spent my entire teaching career introducing students and educators to these principles. The comments at the beginning and end of *MGI I* are from some of our students and professional colleagues. You can have the same kind of impact! Make the words in *My Guide Inside* come alive and use the teacher notes and lesson plans freely.

As a fellow teacher, I invite you, and indeed strongly encourage you to uncover your own guide inside. The words written here, as thoughtfully as they have been prepared for you and your learners, are only an "echo of truth."

Like everyone else in education I also had to find my way. I was a pre-service teacher in 1975 with an up-to-date skill set and a strong desire to help learners who were struggling. Still, I was reconsidering my career choice, because in spite of my desire, I could not reach learners with serious challenges. Try as I might, I could not reach these kids.

What did make the difference? Hearing the truth of these principles. I came to understand the source of natural inner wisdom and well-being; my success rate reaching these learners soared. I had to find "the missing link" for myself, and thus began my lifelong learning journey focused on invigorating the intuitive mind – wisdom – my guide inside.

Knowing about this guide inside is valuable for all learners; however, it is particularly vital for struggling learners. They need knowledge and understanding to experience a healthy life. This curriculum is designed for students with activities that can be graded to report on progress; however, it is also for learners who are curious and whose investigation is not based on a need for grades.

As we learn these principles, we find there is no end to the inner wisdom that brings joy and compassion to life. As author Sydney Banks emphasizes, "Those who have found a balance between their intelligence and their innate wisdom are the lucky ones." (1998, p. 133) Let's be included with the lucky ones!

Make the words in *My Guide Inside* come alive; your success rate and satisfaction will increase profoundly. Ultimately, you will feel better as you experience a new world. As a colleague who wants to share what works without fail, I urge you to please access the included *Recommended Resources* and *Continued Learning for Educators* pages. Please, investigate. These resources are the foundation of *My Guide Inside*. Happy teaching!

Warmest Regards
*Christa Campsall*

*My Guide Inside® (Book I) Teacher's Manual*

## *Overview for Teaching My Guide Inside*

As you prepare to share this curriculum with your students, there are some key considerations that can greatly enhance the support you receive from colleagues and administrators in your school system, and the impact you will have on your students. We have learned over the years the following information can be very beneficial.

❖ **Curriculum Foundations in Research**

Any responsible school curriculum must be built on a solid understanding of current educational research. There are many studies to be considered. (See "*MGI* in Context of Education Theory and Related Research" in this manual for a discussion and detailed listing of related scholarly publications.) For simplicity we have chosen to highlight the work of John Hattie as one sample body of current significant research.

John Hattie holds a PhD from the University of Toronto and is Professor of Education and Director of the Education Research Institute at the University of Melbourne, Australia. He has also served as education professor, administrator, and research director in various universities in Canada, New Zealand, and the United States. He consults globally with key institutions and organizations. Dr. Hattie undertook the largest ever synthesis of meta-analyses of quantitative measures of the effect of different factors on educational outcomes. Hattie is widely published and most known for his Visible Learning books. His quantitative research methodologies document the influences on student achievement described below.

John Hattie and his team by 2015 studied over 1200 meta analyses related to influences on student achievement. These meta analyses examined more than 65,000 studies, 195,000 effect sizes and about ¼ million students worldwide. Hattie aims to discover what maximizes student learning and achievement (Hattie 2015). To answer this question Hattie identifies the greatest to the least effect size resulting from educational program, policy and innovation interventions.

In general, the *Visible Learning* massive global research story uncovered by John Hattie "argues that when teachers see teaching and learning through the eyes of their students, and when students become their own teachers the outcomes and engagement are maximized." (Hattie, 2015, pp. 79).)

A recent report* with rankings, 1.62 to -.42, indicates these are the top three "effects sizes" impacting student achievement:

- **#1—Teacher estimates of student achievement 1.62**
- **#2—Collective teacher efficacy 1.57**
- **#3—Self-reported grades 1.33**

When seen through a Three Principles lens, educators understand these effects this way:

#1 — "Teacher estimates of student achievement" means an individual teacher's view that each student can achieve/learn; with the educator accurately seeing where a student is at present and then having insights revealing how to move the student forward. As Barb Aust writes, "There are no throw away" students and we reach them by "teaching in the moment." (Aust, 2013, 2016.)

#2 — "Collective teacher efficacy" refers to educators in a school or team thinking—being confident—*they can in fact be successful* in teaching and reaching each and every student. They trust each other to add to the development of a solution.

#3 — "Self-reported grades" indicates the degree to which a student knows that he or she is capable of successful learning which becomes self-fulfilling. When a student learns to drop, "I can't learn" thinking, intrinsic motivation propels the student. It is not surprising this effect ranks so highly.

*Additionally*, the most negative influence on student achievement is ***Student Depression with -.42 effect size***. The impact of student well-being on academic achievement could not be clearer!

**What makes a difference?** Student's and teacher's thinking plays a critical role. For example, Hattie writes:

> *"It is less what teachers do in their teaching, but more how they think about their role. It is their mind frames or ways of thinking about teaching and learning that are most critical."* (Hattie, 2015, p. 81)

The *My Guide Inside* curriculum directs teachers and learners beyond believing into knowing this is true—that every student can learn and every teacher can discover insights and wisdom to guide effective teaching. Self-efficacy of both student and teacher come naturally when the inside-out nature of life is discovered.

---

* These rankings are visually available at www.visiblelearning.org/nvd3/visualize/hattie-ranking-interactive-2009-2011-2015.html. It is also important to realize as John Hattie's research continues indefinitely, the precise effect rankings and even definitions of effects will vary slightly. For example, in 2016 Jenni Donohoo describes collective teacher efficacy at 1.57 as the most influential effect (Donohoo, p. 6). Despite various interpretations, we feel key identified factors align well with our Three Principles understanding.

*My Guide Inside® (Book I) Teacher's Manual*

### ❖ Suggestions for Using *My Guide Inside*

*My Guide Inside* is based on three fundamental principles, known as Mind, Consciousness and Thought, that are the foundation of all human experience. These Three Principles, realized and articulated by Sydney Banks, offer a hopeful, simple way for children, youth, and adults to gain understanding of how they operate mentally, from the inside out. This maximizes personal well-being, and improves school climate as well as learner behavior and performance.

*"Mind + Consciousness + Thought = Reality"* (Banks, 2005, p. 42)

This curriculum is most effective when adults who use it are personally familiar with, and living from, these principles and have learned to trust their own guide inside. The common sense of the Three Principles will be natural for students to discover, with the guidance of a principles-based teacher. Every one of us wants to learn and be happy. This is an opportunity for us to also learn from, and with, the students! All instruction aims to measurably impact students and improve their lives. See what kids think: watch the *My Guide Inside* Overview (5min) and *Focus Group Experiences with My Guide Inside* video of secondary student outcomes: 5min summary or full 27min interview myguideinside.com.

### Intended Use

The *MGI* curriculum comprising story-based lessons is designed for use in a school or home or wherever it is important to bring hope to learners. My Guide Inside Learner Book I is designed for student success in this context:

*Reading Level:* "very easy to read" (ages 6-8, Grades 2-3 level)
*Ideal Participation Level:* primary (Grades 2-3); adapt for early primary (Grades K-1)
*Flexibility:* regular course or adapt or modify to suit individual learners
*Settings:* classroom, small group or individual
*Design:* inclusive of self-directed learners working independently
*Digital Media:* Resources at myguideinside.com  password: mgi
   Videos on Demand bring each chapter to life.
*Ideal Time:* start of a program or school year to build community and foster optimism

### Lesson Time Frame

Each of the eight chapters will require two sessions of approximately 30 minutes each. This allows time for: reading, discussion, vocabulary building, reflection and journal entry. Any additional activities chosen, like creative arts and play, will require more time. A wide variety of engaging activities are offered. Chapter 9 offers definitions of *Dandy Words* used in *MGI I*.

### Flexibility and Lessons Plans

The main instructional goal is to have class discussions which foster learner awareness of innate inner wisdom called "my guide inside" in this material. We can discover inner wisdom by sharing big picture ideas. This curriculum is meant as a springboard! The chapters can be used in any order that works for you. You may have your own principles stories to share. Your own insights will lead to a deeper understanding. Be flexible. Follow what you know to do.

The lesson plans do not spell out what to include in a lesson; options are fully provided in the *MGI Learner Book* with stories and activities specific to each lesson. Students may be directed to discussion, vocabulary and journals to expand thinking and communication. *MGI* lesson plans do provide details about how each specific chapter lesson can be aligned with student academic progress. The plans suggest how progress will be accomplished and observed as you carry out the actual lessons. This design achieves an opportunity for teachers to be their own evaluator. As John Hattie so strongly encourages us, "Know thy impact!"

The lesson plans and the *MGI Learner Book* together offer a way of sharing the principles so that student learning in broad important areas—*MGI* objectives for Personal Well-being Awareness and Responsibility—will be achieved. No exhaustive planning is needed, simply read through the logically organized chapters and proceed. For specific details see *Introduction to Objectives and Lesson Plans*. Lessons themselves are easy to use. See *"Come on Along!"* in each lesson plan for a quick overview.

Class sets of *MGI Learner Books* may be used year after year. Alternatively, whenever possible, it is optimal to provide a *MGI Learner Book* for each student to keep and access for further exploration of the key elements.

### Assessment and Observation

All instruction aims to measurably impact students and improve their lives. Three MGI forms, with instructions, are provided in Assessment and Observation. These tools include: Learner MGI I Pre- and Post-Assessments, English Language Arts Assessments, Teacher "Snapshot" Learner Observations. By keeping a copy of each student's Pre- and Post-Assessments, development can be monitored and discussed individually with each learner. **When possible, a school district research office staffer may develop an efficient computerized system for data collection, analysis and reporting to the classroom teacher**. Both individual student and full class reports may be developed.

### Website Supplements for *MGI I*

The *My Guide Inside* website includes the assessment tools: *Learner MGI I Pre- and Post-Assessment, English Language Arts Assessments and Teacher "Snapshot" Learner Observations*. In addition there are Video On Demand classes for each chapter. These classes accompany the *My Guide Inside* Learner book and are designed to be combined with your live online or face to face discussions. Find these supplemental materials on the resources page of the myguideinside.com site. Password: mgi

I am grateful to my colleague Kathy Marshall Emerson, who has introduced Three Principles to literally hundreds of teachers, for clarifying the simplicity of this process in *Educators Living in the Joy of Gratitude*, particularly in Webinar 12. Also see the very helpful book by Barb Aust, *The Essential Curriculum*, in which she beautifully describes what the school and classroom climate is like when the principles are integrated into educational settings. Barb has experience learning, living, and sharing Three Principles during her entire career; she has always shared such wisdom in her roles as teacher, principal and pre-service teacher supervisor. For continued learning see *Supplemental Resources*. These materials will guide you to your own insights.

*My Guide Inside® (Book I) Teacher's Manual*

# Sharing the Principles in Early Childhood Programs

We are often asked, "How can we share the principles with very young children?" We know with certainty, the "essential curriculum" … the teacher living the principles in any classroom, is the most important foundation. We turned to expert Three Principles colleagues for their perspective.

Barb Aust, is a Gulf Islands BC District 64 retired elementary teacher and principal who also developed and managed two daycare centers for 3-6 year olds in British Columbia. She stressed, "The teacher's state of mind and modelling is the most important lesson, for sure! Listen deeply. Find your calm place. Look for treasure [in the children]. Treat them the way you want to be treated."

Dr. Marj Hawkins, retired director of both Early Childhood Family Education and Early Childhood Special Education in St. Cloud Minnesota's District 742 advised: "The *essentials* at the preschool level are experience-based. [They] are not … taught as cognitive learning strategies, but rather, understood by teachers and caregivers. Teachers and caregivers reach children first by developing relationships with them, consequently teaching children self-regulation. There just isn't any other way. Both the initial and ultimate goal for young children is healthy social and emotional development. And the positive outcomes of any healthy relationship are evidenced throughout life. (You like someone, and you perform, even though you might not like the subject matter.)" She continued, "In today's world of challenges, children are often compromised in their developmental trajectory. Achieving social and emotional milestones occurs when kids feel *safe and secure* … then they can learn other things. The teacher/caregiver says " … I will be here with you.' " Dr. Hawkins also relied on a variety of school community support services to bolster children and families in the early years. Many of these professionals have a basic familiarity with the principles.

Barb exuberantly responded to Marj's comments. "Oh my! This is so absolutely right-on! I have always sworn up and down that the best training a teacher can have is to be a preschool or daycare teacher. It is where teachers learn about relationship, ebb and flow, and working as a team where you have to listen from inside as to whether to step forward or back." In early childhood programs, we believe effective teachers and caregivers learn, live and formlessly role model the principles. As preschool children experience that, they do begin to self-regulate rather naturally. This helps prepare youngsters to be able to learn in a more formal way later.

Clearly an early childhood program is not the place for cognitive lessons. The focus is on the essential state of mind the teacher brings to children. Barb Aust's book, *The Essential Curriculum*, is a powerful resource in that regard. There are examples of very young children putting words to the feeling. One parent reported asking, "How did we get such a good boy?" The three-year old replied, "Because you give me so much love." Menomonie, Wisconsin Principal Lori Smith recounts pointing to innate health and the young child declaring, "There are no burned cookies!"

*My Guide Inside®* (Book I) Teacher's Manual

We also know picture books and stories may be well received by preschool children. To that end, Christa Campsall and Jane Tucker have published *Whooo ... Has a Guide Inside?* Parents, early childhood program staffers, and classroom teachers may find this engaging for reading to very young children.

## *Key Teaching Points for Lessons*

**Chapter 1: Discovering My Guide Inside**
You have a guide inside. It is wisdom and common sense.
Everyone has this guide inside. Just look for the feeling.
You can trust your guide. It points you the right way.

**Chapter 2: My Feelings Come from Thought**
My thought creates my feeling.
All of my feelings come from thought.
I let unwanted thought pass by, and well-being is present.

**Chapter 3: Happiness Inside Me**
I listen to my guide inside.
Helpful thoughts pop up.
My good feeling is present again.

**Chapter 4: Fast and Furious or Calm and Curious**
I can see I am thinking fast and furious.
I can choose to let it go.
I can be calm and curious.

**Chapter 5: Enjoying Friendship**
Friends have different ideas.
My guide inside helps me listen to my friend.
We both can have a change of heart.

**Chapter 6: Being A-okay Today**
I can have too much thinking.
I can get stuck on a thought.
I am a-okay with just right thinking.

**Chapter 7: Seeing and Helping Others**
When I am feeling a-okay, my thinking is calm and curious.
I notice when someone needs my help.
My guide inside helps me know what to do.

*My Guide Inside® (Book I) Teacher's Manual*

# Introduction to Objectives and Lesson Plans

The principles discussed in the *My Guide Inside* comprehensive curriculum operate in all people, including students of every age. The Pre-K-12 *MGI* curriculum points the way to wholeness, happiness, creativity and well-being in all parts of life.

Therefore, all lessons in *MGI* Books I, II, and III share two globally appropriate academic objectives to:
(1) **Enhance Personal Well-being with an understanding of these principles**,
(2) **Develop competencies in Communication, Thinking, and Personal and Social Awareness and Responsibility.**

Discovering their *guide inside is* key to learning and **enhances all students' ability to make decisions**, navigate life and **build healthy relationships. Accessing natural wisdom will affect well-being,** spiritual **wellness,** personal and social responsibility, and positive personal and cultural identity. Self-determination, self-regulation and self-efficacy are also natural outcomes of greater awareness.

A guide to *Educational Learning Objectives and Competencies* in all relevant areas is provided below in the section called *Integrating My Guide Inside in Education*. MGI accomplishes its objectives by using age appropriate stories, discussion and various written and creative activities, as it increases competency in English Language Arts and other areas.

*Learner Book I* lesson plans designed to achieve these objectives with primary age students follow.

---

*It may be helpful to know: Each lesson plan contains a brief lesson Orientation for teachers. (This is called "Come on Along!" in the learner book.) The main teaching focus is in bold italics. Especially see the Learner Outcomes placed at the end of each lesson plan. Lesson Aims and Learning Opportunities are also included. In all cases, the first few bulleted items address the chapter's principles lesson. This may help make lessons targeted and possible to fit in into limited class time. Remaining items detail broader learning.*

*My Guide Inside® (Book I) Teacher's Manual*

# Lesson Plan Chapter 1
# Discovering *My Guide Inside*

**Orientation: Come on Along!**

    *On the preceding page of the Learner Book, a mother owl assures her owlets they will know how and when to fly. Like owlets, all children are at promise. The subsequent MGI lessons introduce children to their guide inside, a natural "knowing" available for a lifetime.*

    *Chapter 1 aims for primary children to experientially discover their own guide inside. Key teaching points are:*
1. *You have a guide inside. It is wisdom and common sense.*
2. *Everyone has this guide inside. Just look for the feeling.*
3. *You can trust your guide. It points you the right way.*

    *Students learn to listen to their guide inside and notice what happens when they do. There is wisdom and common sense discoverable by all children. Use the Learner Book riddle, reflections, Evan's story, various Reading Responses, Activity Center, and Dandy Words to aid students in discovering their natural guide inside.*

    ***Remind your students: "You can discover good feelings! You feel secure just being yourself. Notice your guide inside points the way." This enhanced Personal Well-being Awareness assures each learner their guide inside is always available.***

**Chapter Grade Level**

For K and Grade 1 you may consider using only the preface picture page and some activities. Chapter 1 lesson is Grade 2 text, very easy to read. Reader's age is 6-8 years old (Grades 1-2).

**Learner Pre-Assessment**, found in this manual to copy or at [myguideinside.com](http://myguideinside.com), is to be completed prior to this first lesson. A Learner Post-Assessment is completed in the last class.

**Lesson Aims**

Chapter 1 aims for learners to:
- discover their guide inside in these simple terms:
  - You have a guide inside. It is wisdom and common sense.
  - Everyone has this guide inside. Just look for the feeling.
  - You can trust your guide. It points you the right way.

*My Guide Inside® (Book I) Teacher's Manual*

- read and listen to develop personal awareness
- access prior knowledge to make meaning
- express their thoughts and feelings
- increase "knowing myself" by connecting with others
- value themselves and their creative ideas

**Learning Opportunities**

Chapter 1 is designed to encourage learners to:
- gain an understanding of the principles in terms of:
  - beginning to be personally aware of my guide inside and noticing well-being
  - exploring the meaning of my guide inside, also known as wisdom or common sense
- begin to be aware of personal well-being through listening, reading, speaking and writing
- explore and experience the arts to express who they are
- begin to develop respect, fair play and leadership in activities

**Learning Outcomes**

At the end of Chapter 1, learners will show skills and knowledge through:
- an understanding of the principles when
  - describing their own experience noticing their guide inside
  - choosing their own name for their guide inside
  - telling of a time when they felt happy
- participating by listening and reading
- expressing connections between personal experience and text
- showing understanding by creating a journal entry using some conventions
- sharing ideas through the arts
- beginning to demonstrate respect, fair play and leadership in activities

**Resources Tab**

myguideinside.com includes Video On Demand Class to bring this chapter to life.
Password: mgi

**Key Objectives Reminder**

Every chapter has two broad learning objectives: Personal Well-being Awareness and Responsibility. With the special focus of Chapter 1, what do the students tell you they have discovered?

**Activities**

Use *Early or Late Primary Assessment* for English Language Arts (ELA).

*My Guide Inside® (Book I) Teacher's Manual*

# Lesson Plan Chapter 2
# My Feelings Come from Thought

**Orientation: Come on Along!**

In the previous chapter, learners were introduced to their guide inside. Chapter 2 builds on that discovery by exploring the power of each child's thinking to create her or his feelings. A story about twins, Ed and Alice, develops these key teaching points:

1. My thought creates my feeling.
2. All of my feelings come from thought.
3. I let unwanted thoughts pass by and well-being is present.

Using Ed and Alice's examples, students continue noticing the guide inside. They also begin to discover and experience their own thought creating their feelings. Children learn they are creating their own experience.

Use the various Reading Responses for reflective learning, discussion and self-expression. Activities draw on creative and artistic abilities and offer fun play opportunities. Dandy Words enhance vocabulary.

Remind your students: "My feelings come from thought." Their enhanced Personal Awareness ultimately improves self-regulation, self-efficacy, and well-being.

**Chapter Grade Level**

For K and Grade 1 you may consider using only the picture page and some activities. Chapter 2 story is Grade 2 text, very easy to read. Reader's age is 6-8 years old (Grades 1-2).

**Lesson Aims**

Chapter 2 aims for learners to:
- increase an understanding of principles by discovering
  - My thought creates my feeling.
  - All of my feelings come from thought.
  - I let unwanted thoughts pass by and well-being is present.
- read and listen to develop self-awareness
- access prior knowledge to make meaning
- express their thoughts and feelings
- invigorate "knowing myself" by connecting with others
- value themselves and their creative ideas
- understand individuals have their own thoughts and experiences

**Learning Opportunities**
Chapter 2 is designed to encourage learners to:
- gain an understanding of the principles in terms of:
    - beginning to connect thought and feeling
    - knowing freedom from worry
    - enhancing personal well-being and ability to navigate life
- experience and value sharing with a caring adult
- become aware of personal well-being and responsibility by listening, reading, speaking and writing
- beginning to show self-determination and natural self-regulation
- explore and experience the arts to express who they are
- continue to develop respect, fair play and leadership in activities

**Learning Outcomes**
At the end of Chapter 2, learners will show skills and knowledge through:
- an understanding of the principles when:
    - noticing and talking about the relationship of thought to feeling
    - noticing the presence of well-being
- participating by listening and reading
- expressing connections between their personal experience and the story
- showing understanding by creating a journal entry using some conventions
- sharing ideas through the arts
- demonstrating respect, fair play and leadership in activities

**Resources Tab**
myguideinside.com includes Video On Demand Class to bring this chapter to life.
Password: mgi

**Key Objectives Reminder**
Every chapter has two broad learning objectives: Personal Well-being Awareness and Responsibility. With the special focus of Chapter 2, what do the students tell you they have discovered?

**Activities**
Use *Early or Late Primary Assessment* for English Language Arts (ELA).

*My Guide Inside® (Book I) Teacher's Manual*

# Lesson Plan Chapter 3
# Happiness Inside Me

**Orientation: Come on Along!**
   *Previously Chapter 2 introduced learners to the power of thought creating feelings. Chapter 3 explores changes in feelings using the visual metaphor of clouds covering the sun. Gail's story describes losing a good feeling and finding her way back to happiness. These are key teaching points:*
   1. *I listen to my guide inside.*
   2. *Helpful thoughts pop up.*
   3. *My good feeling is present again.*

   *With Gail's example, students continue noticing and discussing their guide inside. They more clearly experience feelings come from thought. New learning involves children beginning to have a very simple ability to notice a change in their own feeling.*

   *Use the various Reading Responses for reflective learning, discussion and self-expression focused on shifts in feeling. The Activity Center uses artistic abilities depicting the sun and clouds to understand losing and regaining a good feeling. A group belly laugh "restores a happy heart." Dandy Words enhance vocabulary.*

   **Remind your students: "What I feel comes from thought."** *This enhanced Personal Awareness ultimately improves well-being and self-efficacy.*

## Chapter Grade Level
For K and Grade 1 you may consider using only the picture page and some activities. Chapter 3 story is Grade 2 text, very easy to read. Reader's age is 6-8 years old (Grades 1-2).

## Lesson Aims
Chapter 3 aims for learners to:
- increase an understanding of principles with these points:
    - I listen to my guide inside.
    - Helpful thoughts pop up.
    - My good feeling is present again.
- read and listen to develop self-awareness
- access prior knowledge to make meaning
- express their thoughts and feelings
- invigorate "knowing myself" by connecting with others
- value themselves and their creative ideas

*My Guide Inside® (Book I) Teacher's Manual*

**Learning Opportunities**
Chapter 3 is designed to encourage learners to:
- gain an understanding of the principles in terms of:
  - gaining awareness that happiness and well-being are inside
  - experiencing insightful thought creating positive feeling
  - realizing kindness supports others' shift to inner happiness and well-being
- begin to value positive relationships
- begin to develop awareness of personal well-being and responsibility through listening, reading, speaking and writing
- begin to develop awareness of self-determination and natural self-regulation
- build relationships, work or play co-operatively, solve problems peacefully
- explore and experience the arts to express who they are
- develop respect, fair play and leadership in activities

**Learning Outcomes**
At the end of Chapter 3, learners will show skills and knowledge through:
- an understanding of the principles when
  - reporting on listening to their guide inside
  - experiencing happiness
  - noticing state of mind shifts
- participating by listening and reading
- expressing connections between personal experience and story
- showing understanding by creating a journal entry using some conventions
- sharing ideas through the arts
- demonstrating respect, fair play and leadership in activities

**Resources Tab**
myguideinside.com includes Video On Demand Class to bring this chapter to life.
Password: mgi

**Key Objectives Reminder**
Every chapter has two broad learning objectives: Personal Well-being Awareness and Responsibility. With the special focus of Chapter 3, what do the students tell you they have discovered?

**Activities**
Use *Early or Late Primary Assessment* for English Language Arts (ELA).

> NOTE: This quotation appears in Chapter 3: "Happy thoughts bring happy days and sad thoughts bring sad days." The source is *Dear Liza* by Sydney Banks page 51.

*My Guide Inside® (Book I) Teacher's Manual*

# Lesson Plan Chapter 4
# Fast and Furious or Calm and Curious

**Orientation: Come on Along!**
   *Previously Chapter 3 introduced learners to noticing changes in their feelings. Chapter 4 prepares learners to notice changes in the quality of their thinking. Kayla's story portrays "tornado thinking" as fast and furious. She learns to let thoughts go and naturally shift to calm and curious thinking.* These are key teaching points:
   1. *I can see I am thinking fast and furious.*
   2. *I can choose to let it go.*
   3. *I can be calm and curious.*

   *With Kayla's example, as with previous lessons, students are frequently listening to, and discussing, their guide inside and understanding thought creates all of their feelings. Learners have a budding ability to notice changes in their own thoughts and feelings.*

   *Use the various Reading Responses to facilitate discussion, increase communication and understanding. The Activity Center uses art and play to create opportunities for learners to see the quality of their own thought in action. Dandy Words support vocabulary enhancement and communication progress.*

   *Remind your students: "I can spy a tornado! I know what to do." This enhanced Personal Well-being Awareness greatly improves self-regulation and social responsibility.*

**Chapter Grade Level**
For K and Grade 1 you may consider using only the picture page and some activities. Chapter 4 story is Grade 3 text, very easy to read. Reader's age is 7-9 years old (Grades 2-3).

**Lesson Aims**
Chapter 4 aims for learners to:
- increase an understanding of principles with these points:
    - I can see I am thinking fast and furious.
    - I can choose to let it go.
    - I can be calm and curious.
- read and listen to develop self-awareness
- access prior knowledge to make meaning
- express their thoughts and feelings
- invigorate "knowing myself and my world" by connecting with others
- value themselves and their creative ideas

*My Guide Inside® (Book I) Teacher's Manual*

**Learning Opportunities**
Chapter 4 is designed to encourage learners to:
- gain an understanding of the principles in terms of:
  - experiencing the difference between fast and furious, and calm and curious thinking
  - connecting with their inner wisdom to make wise choices
  - experiencing the healthy choice of letting thoughts go, dropping thoughts
  - realizing the impact of thought choices on well-being of self and others
- develop awareness of personal well-being and responsibility by listening, reading, speaking and writing
- develop self-determination and natural control of impulses regulating behavior
- explore and experience the arts to express who they are
- develop respect, fair play and leadership in activities

**Learning Outcomes**
At the end of Chapter 4, learners will show skills and knowledge through:
- an understanding of the principles when:
  - being aware of good choices
  - contrasting fast and furious thinking, with calm and curious thinking
- participating by listening and reading
- expressing connections between personal experience and story
- revealing understanding by creating a journal entry using some conventions
- sharing ideas through the arts
- demonstrating respect, fair play and leadership in activities

**Resources Tab**
myguideinside.com includes Video On Demand Class to bring this chapter to life.
Password: mgi

**Key Objectives Reminder**
Every chapter lesson has two broad learning objectives: Personal Well-being Awareness and Responsibility. With the special focus of Chapter 4, what do the students tell you they have discovered?

**Activities**
Use *Early or Late Primary Assessment* for English Language Arts (ELA).

*My Guide Inside® (Book I) Teacher's Manual*

## Lesson Plan Chapter 5
## Enjoying Friendship

**Orientation: Come on Along!**

*Previously Chapter 4 introduced learners to noticing changes in the quality of their thinking. Chapter 5 focuses on students* learning to maintain friendships. *Daniel and Jason's story describes challenges they face because they think differently. They both learn to listen to their guide inside. In doing so, they are able to accept their separate realities and make new plans for a sleepover. Key teaching points in this chapter are:*

1. *Friends have different ideas.*
2. *My guide inside helps me listen to my friend.*
3. *We both can have a change of heart.*

*As in previous lessons, during Daniel and Jason's story, learners gain experience listening to their guide inside, knowing thought creates all their feelings, noticing when they lose a good feeling, and naming the quality of their thinking. Chapter 5 brings a new lesson: Wise friends have different ideas, can listen to each other, and experience a change of heart.*

*Use the various Reading Responses to gain deeper understanding. Writer's Workshop interviews and writing strengthen communication and self-expression. Activity Center art and play expands listening, communication and highlights the role of wisdom in friendships. Dandy Words fosters descriptive abilities.*

*Remind your students: "I can listen to you. We both can decide to change a little." This enhanced Personal Well-being Awareness builds healthy relationships and increases social responsibility.*

**Chapter Grade Level**

For K and Grade 1 you may consider using only the picture page and some activities. Chapter 5 story is Grade 3 text, very easy to read. Reader's age is 7-9 years old (Grades 2-3).

**Lesson Aims**

Chapter 5 aims for learners to:
- increase an understanding of principles with these points:
    - Friends have different ideas.
    - My guide inside helps me listen to my friend.
    - We both can have a change of heart.
- read and listen to develop self-awareness of self and friends
- access prior knowledge to make meaning of enjoying friendship

*My Guide Inside® (Book I) Teacher's Manual*

- express their thoughts and feelings about wise friendship
- invigorate "knowing myself and my world" by listening to friends
- value themselves and their creative ideas in the context of friendship

**Learning Opportunities**
Chapter 5 is designed to encourage learners to:
- gain an understanding of the principles in terms of:
  - identifying opportunities to make healthy decisions
  - listening to inner wisdom to make healthy friendship decisions
  - discovering friends can change their mind and solve problems peacefully
- continue to develop awareness of personal well-being and responsibility in friendships by listening, reading, speaking and writing
- increase awareness of self-determination and natural self-regulation
- explore and experience the arts to express who they are as a friend
- increase respect, fair play and leadership in activities

**Learning Outcomes**
At the end of Chapter 5, learners will show skills and knowledge through:
- an understanding of the principles when:
  - using their guide inside to make and keep friendships
  - responding to friends with calm and curious thinking
  - having perspective and realizing together friends can agree to change their minds
- participating by listening and reading
- expressing connections between personal experience and story
- working and playing with friends collaboratively for mutual benefit
- demonstrating understanding of wise friendship by writing, editing and sharing a story
- sharing ideas about healthy friendship through the arts
- demonstrating respect, fair play and leadership

**Resources Tab**
myguideinside.com includes Video On Demand Class to bring this chapter to life.
Password: mgi

**Key Objectives Reminder**
Every chapter has two broad learning objectives: Personal Well-being Awareness and Responsibility. With the special focus of Chapter 5, what do the students tell you they have discovered?

**Activities**
Use *Early or Late Primary Assessment* for English Language Arts (ELA).

*My Guide Inside® (Book I) Teacher's Manual*

# Lesson Plan Chapter 6
# Being A-okay Today

**Orientation: Come on Along!**

*Learners were already introduced, in Chapter 5, to following their guide inside in order to enjoy friendships. Chapter 6 prepares learners to notice how they are doing so they can be at their best with just right thinking. Amy's story portrays her feeling apprehensive and anxious while visiting an unfamiliar park. An older cousin, Ella, helps Amy notice her state of mind. Amy discovers she can enjoy playing with kids she does not know. Key teaching points in this chapter are:*

1. *I can have too much thinking.*
2. *I can get stuck on a thought.*
3. *I am a-okay with just right thinking.*

*During Amy's story, learners again gain experience listening to their own guide inside, knowing thought creates all feelings, noticing when they lose a good feeling and seeing the quality of their thinking. Chapter 6 prepares young learners to begin to notice their state of mind and naturally self-correct.*

*Opportunities for this learning are presented in Reading Responses, Writer's Workshop, Poetry Café, Art Activities, and Dandy Words.*

*Remind your students: "I can notice how I am doing. My thinking can be just right, a-okay." Self-regulation and self-efficacy are natural outcomes. This enhanced Personal Well-being Awareness develops competencies in thinking, communication, and social responsibility.*

**Chapter Grade Level**

For K and Grade 1 you may consider using only the picture page and some activities. Chapter 6 story is Grade 3 text, very easy to read. Reader's age is 7-9 years old (Grades 2-3).

**Lesson Aims**

Chapter 6 aims for learners to:
- increase an understanding of principles with these points:
  – I can have too much thinking.
  – I can get stuck on a thought.
  – I am a-okay with just right thinking.
- read and listen to develop self-awareness
- access prior knowledge to make meaning

*My Guide Inside® (Book I) Teacher's Manual*

- express their thoughts and feelings
- invigorate "knowing myself and my world" by connecting with others
- value themselves and their creative ideas

## Learning Opportunities
Chapter 6 is designed to encourage learners to:
- gain an understanding of the principles in terms of:
  - noticing too much thinking or stuck state of mind
  - trusting just right thinking leads to happiness
  - experiencing the self-correcting power of listening to the guide inside for insight
  - feeling I'm a-okay now (back in a state of well-being)
  - listening to the guide inside naturally
- deepen personal awareness of well-being and responsibility for their own happiness by listening, reading, speaking and writing
- increase self-determination and natural self-regulation
- explore and experience the arts to more fully and confidently express who they are
- increase respect, fair play and leadership in activities
- write poems, edit and recite a poem fluently

## Learning Outcomes
At the end of Chapter 6, learners will show skills and knowledge through:
- an understanding of the principles when
  - assessing their own state of mind
  - using "just right thinking" to be a-okay
  - making healthy decisions
  - knowing to be calm and curious before making choices
  - using insights and new ideas effectively
- participating by listening, reading and reciting
- expressing connections between personal experience and story
- recognizing and accepting support
- showing understanding through writing, editing and reciting a poem
- sharing ideas through the arts
- demonstrate respect, co-operation and leadership in activities

## Resources Tab
myguideinside.com includes Video On Demand Class to bring this chapter to life. Password: mgi

## Key Objectives Reminder
Every chapter has two broad learning objectives: Personal Well-being Awareness and Responsibility. With the special focus of Chapter 6, what do the students tell you they have discovered?

## Activities
Use *Early or Late Primary Assessment* for English Language Arts (ELA).

*My Guide Inside® (Book I) Teacher's Manual*

# Lesson Plan Chapter 7
# Seeing and Helping Others

**Orientation: Come on Along!**

*Learners were already introduced, in Chapter 6, to noticing how they are doing so they can be at their best—a-okay—with just right thinking. Chapter 7 prepares students to see when other children or adults are not a-okay and need help. Owen and Nathan's story focuses on their friendship and common interest in soccer. Owen listens to the guide inside and realizes Nathan, who is two years younger, is unsure about his ability to learn to play on a team. Owen helps Nathan be calm and curious before deciding to quit or stay on the team. Key teaching points in this chapter are:*

1. *When I am a-okay, my thinking is calm and curious.*
2. *I notice when someone needs my help.*
3. *My guide inside helps me know what to do.*

*Remind your students, "If I am a-okay, I can spot when someone is not. If I listen to the guide inside I will know what to do." Focus of this lesson is on building healthy relationships by being sensitive and helpful to others.*

**Chapter Grade Level**

For K and Grade 1 you may consider using only the picture page and some activities. Chapter 7 story is Grade 2 text, very easy to read. Reader's age is 6-8 years old (Grades 1-2).

**Lesson Aims**

Chapter 7 aims for learners to:
- increase an understanding of the principles with these points:
  - When I am a-okay, my thinking is calm and curious.
  - I notice when someone needs my help.
  - My guide inside helps me know what to do.
- read and listen to develop self-awareness
- access prior knowledge to make meaning
- express their thoughts and feelings
- invigorate "knowing myself and my world" by being aware of, and helping others
- value themselves and their creative ideas

*My Guide Inside® (Book I) Teacher's Manual*

**Learning Opportunities**
Chapter 7 is designed to encourage learners to:
- gain an understanding of the principles in terms of:
  - beginning to assess and maintain their own well-being, (being a-okay)
  - using their guide inside to be aware of others and their needs
  - relying on insights to guide them in knowing what to do for others
- continue to deepen personal well-being awareness and responsibility through listening, reading, speaking and writing
- continue to deepen awareness of self-determination and natural self-regulation
- explore and experience the arts to express who they are in relation to others
- develop respect, fair play and leadership in activities with others
- write *My Storybook*, edit with support and read the story fluently

**Learning Outcomes**
At the end of Chapter 7, learners will show skills and knowledge through:
- an understanding of the principles when:
  - noticing others in need of help
  - being naturally motivated to help others in need
  - being calm and curious—responsible—in choosing how to help or get help
- participating by listening and reading to others
- taking responsibility for their environments by playing collaboratively
- expressing connections between personal experience and story
- showing understanding through writing, editing and sharing *My Storybook*
- artistically expressing ideas about helping others
- demonstrating respect, fair play and leadership in activities

**Resources Tab**
myguideinside.com includes Video On Demand Class to bring this chapter to life.
Password: mgi

**Key Objectives Reminder**
Every chapter has two broad learning objectives: Personal Well-being Awareness and Responsibility. With the special focus of Chapter 7, what do the students tell you they have discovered?

**Activities**
Use *Early or Late Primary Assessment* for English Language Arts (ELA).

*My Guide Inside® (Book I) Teacher's Manual*

# Lesson Plan Chapter 8
# Knowing Myself

**Orientation: Come on Along!**

*Learners were already introduced in, Chapter 7, to noticing and helping other children in need. Chapter 8 is a review of what they have learned from My Guide Inside. In this reflection they are encouraged to keep listening to their guide inside. They will know when they are a-okay and when they are not. Feelings will be their guide. It is important to be calm and curious and watch for passing thought tornados. Learners learned too much thinking passes like clouds covering the sun. The sun always comes out with "just right thinking." It will be helpful to remember friends can have different ideas and listening brings a change of heart. Being a-okay makes it easy to be friendly, kind and helpful to others. The guide inside is always present. With this wisdom, children can learn to walk through life as a happy person.*

*Remind your students: "Your guide inside points you in the right direction. You can be a-okay today." This final lesson focuses on review and reflection. Learners describe in their own words what they learned and find important to remember. Ultimately listening to the guide inside becomes a way of life. Personal awareness and responsibility are natural outcomes.*

**Chapter Grade Level**

Chapter 8 lesson is Grade 3 text, very easy to read. Reader's age is 7-9 years old (Grades 2-3). For K and Grade 1 you may consider using only the final picture page and some activities. **Learner Post-Assessment**, found in this manual or at myguideinside.com, is to be completed at the end of this last lesson. See additional details below.

Key teaching points for all chapters are listed below to support student reflection and discussion. These may also be helpful as students begin work on activities listed below.

**Chapter 1 Discovering My Guide Inside**
- You have a guide inside. It is wisdom and common sense.
- Everyone has this guide inside. Just look for the feeling.
- You can trust your guide. It points you the right way.

**Chapter 2 My Feelings Come from Thought**
- My thought creates my feeling.
- All of my feelings come from thought.
- I let unwanted thought pass by and well-being is present.

**Chapter 3 Happiness Inside Me**
- I listen to my guide inside.
- Helpful thoughts pop up.
- My good feeling is present again.

**Chapter 4 Fast and Furious or Calm and Curious**
- I can see I am thinking fast and furious.
- I can choose to let it go.
- I can be calm and curious.

**Chapter 5 Enjoying Friendship**
- Friends have different ideas.
- My guide inside helps me listen to my friend.
- We both can have a change of heart.

**Chapter 6 Being A-okay Today**
- I can have too much thinking.
- I can get stuck on a thought.
- I am a-okay with just right thinking.

**Chapter 7 Seeing and Helping Others**
- When I am a-okay, my thinking is calm and curious.
- I notice when someone needs my help.
- My guide inside helps me know what to do.

**Lesson Aims**
Chapter 8 aims for learners to:
- solidify their understanding of the principles by:
  - reflecting on their *My Guide Inside* learning journey
  - using their own words to report what is important to them
- read and listen to each other to develop self-awareness and interest in others
- access prior knowledge to make meaning
- express their thoughts and feelings in their own words
- invigorate "knowing myself and my world" by sharing with others
- value themselves and their creative ideas
- identify personal well-being and their circle of support

### Learning Opportunities
Chapter 8 is designed to encourage learners to:
- clarify and personalize an understanding of the principles by:
    - reflecting on what they have learned from studying *My Guide Inside*
    - reflecting on their ability and circle of support
- reflect on personal well-being awareness and responsibility through listening, reading, speaking and writing
- reflect on awareness of self-determination and natural self-regulation
- use the arts to express who they are
- recognize their own wisdom and identify personal ability to do well

### Learning Outcomes
At the end of Chapter 8, learners will show skills and knowledge through:
- an understanding of the principles when:
    - demonstrating awareness of wisdom and confidence
    - taking responsibility for own choices
    - describing feeling a-okay
    - using key lessons learned from *MGI*
    - using some favorite terms they have learned or created
- recognizing and accepting support
- seeing a need and providing support to others
- participating by listening and reading
- showing understanding through creating a personal metaphor

### Resources Tab
myguideinside.com includes Video On Demand Class to bring this chapter to life. Password: mgi

### Activities
Use *Early or Late Primary Assessment* for English Language Arts (ELA).

### Post-Assessment and Observation
Complete the *Learner Post-Assessment* in the last class. Compare this with each learner's *Pre-Assessment*. There is also a *Teacher Snapshot Observation* available. Both forms may be discussed individually with students, and/or, their parents at an appropriate time. General results may also be shared with the class after *MGI* is completed. Observations can be used for report card comments as needed.

### Celebrate Completing *MGI*
Create and enjoy a special time together in the classroom. Make this fun and inclusive.

**Final Note to Teachers**

When you have completed this class do take time to reflect on what you have done well and what you might try in the future. Especially pay attention to what your own wisdom reveals about your teaching experience with *My Guide Inside*. How has it impacted not only your students, but you yourself? Sydney Banks advises us to "exercise our choice and find inner wisdom for ourselves." Once found, we naturally share and we are advised by John Hattie to "Know thy impact!"

*Congratulations on making a difference in the world!*

**NOTE:** The quotation in *Learner Book I*, Chapter 8, "... you can walk through life as a happy person ..." is from the Sydney Banks DVD, *Long Beach Lecture #4*, 2000

*My Guide Inside® (Book I) Teacher's Manual*

# Lesson Plan Chapter 9
# Dandy Words

**Orientation: Come on Along!**

*Chapter 9 is the final chapter in MGI I. It lists important vocabulary building Dandy Words used in each of the preceding chapters. Refer learners to these pages to find the meaning of these key words and develop their expressive language. Chapter word lists may also be used as thought starters for small discussion groups and written reflections or other age appropriate activities.*

*Remind your students: "Listen to your guide inside. Use your own words!" Students will have their own meaningful words to communicate their awareness of personal well-being, responsibility and relationships with others.*

**Unique Class Words**

Consider the terms that have become favorites in your *MGI* class. Also make a list of those words that are special and unique to your class' understanding of the principles. Use those words in final review with the students. We find every class comes up with some descriptive words about the principles that have special meaning for them.

Before facilitating review or use of words, also glance through the *Dandy Words* found in Chapter 9 of the *Learner Book*.

**Additional Resources**

After completing *MGI*, you might want to follow up with the picture book, *Whooo ... Has a Guide Inside?* by Christa Campsall and Jane Tucker, listed in *Supplemental Resources*. In addition, as a classroom teacher, you may find your own favorite books to continue sharing the principles introduced in *My Guide Inside*. The principles are elemental and often easily discerned in your own favorite books, stories and videos.

## Assessment and Observation

**First Class:**

- Learners complete the *MGI I Pre- and Post-Assessment* prior to the first lesson. Please ensure students understand how to complete the assessment. Provide reading support as needed.

**All Classes:**

- Teacher uses appropriate criteria from *English Language Arts Assessments*.

**Final Class:**

- Learners repeat the *MGI Post-Assessment*.

Teacher completes *"Snapshot" Learner Observations*.

Teacher and students compare *Learner Pre- and Post-Assessment* results and discuss highlights of these outcomes. This may be done individually or as a group. Especially note increased personal awareness, understanding well-being and responsibility. Conclude with a celebration and commitment to use my guide inside throughout life. (Teachers included!)

**Special Notes:**
**When possible, a school district research office staffer may develop an efficient computerized system for** *Pre- and Post-Assessment* **data collection, analysis and reporting to the classroom teacher.** Both individual student and full class digital reports may be developed. It may be helpful to share results with appropriate school building or district officials for purposes of program evaluation and planning.

PDF's of these assessment and observations forms are located at myguideinside.com

**Learner *MGI* Pre- and Post Assessment**
Class_____ID_____Date_____

Circle what you think before the first chapter and do the same after the last chapter!

| Circle the answer that is true for you | Almost Never | A Little | Some | Mostly | A Lot |
|---|---|---|---|---|---|
| 1. I am happy. | Almost Never | A Little | Some | Mostly | A Lot |
| 2. I can wait for good ideas to pop into my head. | Almost Never | A Little | Some | Mostly | A Lot |
| 3. When I worry I let it go. | Almost Never | A Little | Some | Mostly | A Lot |
| 4. It is easy for me to keep friends. | Almost Never | A Little | Some | Mostly | A Lot |
| 5. I think too much. | Almost Never | A Little | Some | Mostly | A Lot |
| 6. I like myself. | Almost Never | A Little | Some | Mostly | A Lot |
| 7. When I get upset I can get over it. | Almost Never | A Little | Some | Mostly | A Lot |
| 8. I am a good learner. | Almost Never | A Little | Some | Mostly | A Lot |

What did you learn from *My Guide Inside* that helped you the most?

*My Guide Inside® (Book I) Teacher's Manual*

# Teacher "Snapshot" Learner Observations

*Prior to completing this form, review each student's progress based on a comparison of their Pre- to Post- Assessments. Reflect and then complete this "Snapshot" to record your main observations. Take time with each student to hear his or her sense of personal progress. Then share your observations. Use for reporting as needed.*

Name: _____   Date: _____

<u>*PERSONAL WELL-BEING AWARENESS*</u> (I listen to my guide inside. I am a-okay.)

    Almost Never    **1**    **2**    **3**    **4**    **5**    A Lot

**Observations:**


<u>*COMMUNICATION, THINKING, PERSONAL AND SOCIAL RESPONSIBILITY*</u>
(I know my thoughts, writing and art have value. I listen to others. I see and help others.)

    Almost Never    **1**    **2**    **3**    **4**    **5**    A Lot

**Observations:**


<u>*RELEVANT STUDENT INFORMATION*</u>

**School Attendance**
Not yet within Expectations    1    2    3    4    5    Fully Meets Expectations

**Classroom academic performance**
Not yet within Expectations    1    2    3    4    5    Fully Meets Expectations

**Social behavior in and out of classroom**
Not yet within Expectations    1    2    3    4    5    Fully Meets Expectations

**Participation in class**
Not yet within Expectations    1    2    3    4    5    Fully Meets Expectations

**Observations:**

*My Guide Inside® (Book I) Teacher's Manual*

# Early Primary Assessment for English Language Arts

The following criteria are for English Language Arts Competencies adapted from *British Columbia's New Curriculum* https://curriculum.gov.bc.ca/ *MGI* stories are meant to educate, foster insight and provide enjoyment. Criteria are provided to use as assessment *for* learning, or as assessment *of* learning for reporting purposes. This assessment includes what the student can do, as well as the next step for learning.

**Name**_____ **Date** _____ **Activity** _____

### Early Primary Reading, Listening Criteria
Early primary students (Pre-K-, K, Grade 1) fully meeting expectations can:
- read simple familiar texts fluently (Yes or Not Yet)
- create reading response, make personal meaning using prior knowledge (Yes or Not Yet)
- make simple inferences (Yes or Not Yet)
- engage actively to develop understanding of self (Yes or Not Yet)
- show respect to the speaker (Yes or Not Yet)

**Comment on next learning steps for Reading, Listening:**


### Early Primary Writing, Speaking, Representing Criteria
Early primary students (Pre-K, K, Grade 1) fully meeting expectations can:
- take turns sharing ideas to build understanding (Yes or Not Yet)
- present ideas (Yes or Not Yet)
- develop word knowledge (Yes or Not Yet)
- create texts to enhance self-awareness in journal, poem, or story (Yes or Not Yet)
- use some conventions of spelling, grammar and punctuation (Yes or Not Yet)
- communicate in a variety of ways for different purposes and audiences (Yes or Not Yet)

**Comment on next learning steps for Writing, Speaking, Representing:**

*My Guide Inside® (Book I) Teacher's Manual*

# Late Primary Assessment for English Language Arts

The following criteria are for English Language Arts Competencies adapted from *British Columbia's New Curriculum* at https://curriculum.gov.bc.ca/ *MGI* stories are meant to educate, foster insight and provide enjoyment. Criteria are provided to use as assessment *for* learning, or as assessment *of* learning for reporting purposes. This assessment includes what the student can do, as well as the next step for learning.

**Name**_____ **Date** _____ **Activity** _____

### Late Primary Reading, Listening Criteria
Late primary students (Grades 2 and 3) fully meeting expectations can:
- read fluently at grade level (Yes or Not Yet)
- create reading responses (Yes or Not Yet)
- make meaning using prior knowledge and sources of information (Yes or Not Yet)
- make connections to build understanding (Yes or Not Yet)
- engage actively offering ideas and opinions to deepen self-awareness (Yes or Not Yet)
- respect others' contributions (Yes or Not Yet)

**Comment on next learning steps for Reading, Listening:**



### Late Primary Writing, Speaking, Representing Criteria
Late primary students (Grades 2 and 3) fully meeting expectations can:
- offer ideas and share opinions to build understanding (Yes or Not Yet)
- ask questions (Yes or Not Yet)
- develop word knowledge (Yes or Not Yet)
- create texts to deepen self-awareness in journal, poem, story (Yes or Not Yet)
- use most conventions of spelling, grammar and punctuation (Yes or Not Yet)
- plan, create varied communications for different purposes, audiences (Yes or Not Yet)

**Comment on next learning steps for Writing, Speaking, Representing:**

*My Guide Inside® (Book I) Teacher's Manual*

## Integrating My Guide Inside in Education

Undoubtedly, as an educator you are responsible for meeting official learning objectives and student competency standards. *My Guide Inside* is designed to help you do that. *My Guide Inside* meets educational learning objectives and competency requirements.

**Current Education Policy Context**
As we write this *Teacher's Manual*, the British Columbia Ministry of Education in Canada is developing a new curriculum including, "Personal Awareness and Responsibility Competence Profile." *MGI* aligns with these innovative guidelines.

The most current version of that work states, "Personal awareness and responsibility is one of the three interrelated competencies that relate to the broad area of Social and Emotional Learning." The curriculum further explains Personal Awareness and Responsibility competency involves: Self-determination, Self-regulation, and Well-being. The Ministry discusses Well-being this way:

> *"Students who are personally aware and responsible recognize how their decisions and actions affect their mental, physical, emotional, social, cognitive, and spiritual wellness, and take increasing responsibility for caring for themselves. They keep themselves healthy and physically active, manage stress, and express a sense of personal well-being. … They recognize the importance of happiness, and have strategies that help them find peace in challenging situations."*

*(Personal Awareness and Responsibility Competence Profiles, p. 3)*

There is also an interest in promoting well-being in the United Kingdom's schools. According to "Promoting Fundamental British Values as part of SMSC in Schools," schools must "promote the spiritual, moral, social and cultural (SMSC) development of their pupils." At this time there is increasing awareness globally of the need for all education systems to support and foster lifelong well-being of students. In that sense this comprehensive Pre-K-12 *My Guide Inside* curriculum is a timely resource for all educators and their school systems.

*Regardless of where you are located in the world, this material is suited for and meets selected requirements for English Language Arts (ELA), Health Education, Career Education, and Personal, Social, Health and Economic Education (PSHE). It supports inclusion and may be used to develop competencies in Communication (C), Thinking (T) and Social Emotional Learning (SEL), which includes decision making, self-management, healthy relationships and well-being. It also may be used to develop competencies in Personal and Social Responsibility (PS), which includes positive personal and cultural identity, personal awareness and responsibility, spiritual wellness, as well as social awareness and responsibility.*

Learners everywhere can discover the guide inside, also referred to simply as common sense or wisdom. They become increasingly aware of and take responsibility for thoughts and actions that impact their intellectual, creative, social, emotional and physical potentials as well as their spiritual wellness. Accessing natural inner wisdom produces joy, love, compassion, personal strength, and leads to academic success. The principles on which this curriculum is based are the key to innate mental health characterized by optimism, resilience, and well-being.

Understanding these principles actually supports and increases a student's well-being, self-efficacy and self-confidence; and improves ability to self-regulate, set goals, and take responsibilities for their choices and actions. With understanding, students become patient learning over time, persevere in difficult situations to solve problems calmly, and realize the logic of how their actions affect themselves and others.

### **Objectives of *My Guide Inside***

The principles discussed in the *My Guide Inside* comprehensive curriculum operate in all people, including students of every age. The Pre-K-12 MGI curriculum points the way to wholeness, happiness, creativity and well-being in all parts of life.

Therefore, all lessons in *MGI* Books I, II, and III share two globally appropriate academic objectives to: **(1) Enhance Personal Well-being with an understanding of these principles**, and **(2) Develop competencies in Communication, Thinking, and Personal and Social Awareness and Responsibility.**

Discovering their guide inside is key to learning and **enhances every students' ability to make decisions, navigate life and build healthy relationships.** *MGI* accomplishes its objectives by using age appropriate stories, discussion and various written and creative activities, as it increases competency in English Language Arts.

*My Guide Inside® (Book I) Teacher's Manual*

# Educational Learning Objectives and Competencies

*My Guide Inside curriculum also meets these additional requirements common to most school systems globally as detailed below.*

### English Language Arts Objectives

**Reading and Viewing:** Learners will expand their knowledge and apply strategies to understand, compare ideas with prior knowledge, make inferences, reflect, and respond. Learners will enhance their vocabulary while they read and view for enjoyment, to explore ideas and to inspire creativity. They will synthesize texts to create insight and communicate viewpoints to expand thinking.

**Writing and Representation:** : Learners will expand their communication and create meaningful texts, including visual texts, that show depth of thought and have a logical sequence. Learners will refine texts with enhanced vocabulary, clear language and some correct conventions of grammar, spelling and punctuation. Learners will use an engaging "voice" and present texts in a variety of ways.

**Oral Language:** Listening and speaking are foundations of language learning for developing vocabulary, making connections and having perspective. Learners will expand knowledge by listening to others as well as realizing what they themselves know by reflecting, expressing their own point of view and communicating through oral language. Learners will rehearse and perform to produce language and discuss language meaning.

### Career Education and Health Education Objectives

Learners will develop confidence through the process of self-discovery. Learners will respond suitably to discrimination and harassment, show respect and understand what makes and maintains a healthy relationship. Learners will identify supportive relationships, healthy thoughts and feelings, and understand personal safety. Learners will access knowledge to support healthy decisions.

### Communication Competency

Learners will share with others in conversation to develop understanding and relationships. Learners will communicate and collaborate on activities, including effective use of Digital Media, to present their work. Students will acquire knowledge and share what they have learned through presentations, self-monitoring and self-assessment.

### Personal and Social Competencies (Social and Emotional Learning)

**Personal Responsibility:** Learners can anticipate results of own actions. They understand and become increasingly aware of and take responsibility for thoughts and actions that impact their intellectual, creative, social, emotional and physical potentials, as well as their spiritual wellness. They are flexible; making responsible decisions about which thoughts to act on, based on well-being of self and others.

- **Well-being**: Through an understanding of my guide inside, ever-present natural inner wisdom or common sense, learners take increasing responsibility for their personal well-being, which includes their safety and happiness. Learners understand that mental health is a state of well-being.
- **Self-Determination:** Learners understand the cause and effect rule that thought creates feeling and thought is the "seed" of behavior. Learners have confidence, an awareness of strengths to face challenges and know to access compassion. Learners advocate for themselves.
- **Self-Regulation:** Learners choose their guide inside (their own natural inner wisdom) to regulate behavior effectively and control impulses. Learners show honesty, motivate themselves and work toward achieving success.

**Social Awareness and Responsibility:** Learners are fair, appreciate others' perspectives and solve problems in peaceful ways. They show empathy, compassion and understanding, and are inclusive and contribute to the community.

- **Healthy Relationships:** Learners listen, co-operate and communicate clearly. They show compassion, empathy and understanding, solve people problems calmly, and seek and offer help when needed.

**Positive Personal and Cultural Identity**: Learners understand their identity evolves as they gain understanding and experience in life. Learners see that natural inner wisdom combined with personal attributes can help them navigate life. Learners identify people who can support them as well as see that they can also offer help.

*Thinking Competency*

Learners will gain awareness of the power of thought, which is the thinking process in action. Via creative thinking, they will generate ideas while investigating relevance and connection to "Big Picture" ideas. They will learn that their ideas have value. Learners will understand to let the personal mind clear to allow new thought to emerge. They will have opportunities to develop new ideas, insights, that change what they do in life. Via reflective and critical thinking, learners will choose which thoughts to pay attention to, which logically lead to intended outcomes.

*My Guide Inside® (Book I) Teacher's Manual*

## *Supplemental Resources*

### *Recommended Three Principles Resources*

**By Sydney Banks:**
**Books**
*Second Chance* (1983)
*In Quest of the Pearl* (1989)
*The Missing Link: Reflections on Philosophy and Spirit* (1998)
*The Enlightened Gardener* (2001)
*Dear Liza* (2004)
*The Enlightened Gardener Revisited* (2005)
**CDs**

| | | |
|---|---|---|
| *Attitude!* | *In Quest of the Pearl* | *Second Chance* |
| *Great Spirit, The* | *Long Beach Lectures* | *Washington Lectures* |
| *Hawaii Lectures* | *One Thought Away* | *What is Truth* |

**DVDs**
*Hawaii Lectures (1-4)*
*Long Beach Lectures (1-4)*
*Washington Lectures (1-2)*
*The Ultimate Answer*

See www.sydbanks.com and Sydney Banks Videos: https://www.youtube.com/@sydney-banks3/videos

### *Continued Learning for Educators*

*The Power of the Three Principles in Schools* four-part free online professional development series for educators created by Christa Campsall and Barb Aust. This series links to Sydney Banks *Long Beach* Lectures.
www.myguideinside.com

***Long Beach Lectures (1-4)*** video series of presentations by Sydney Banks
www.sydbanks.com/longbeach/

Marshall K. (2021). ***Discovering Resilience and Well-being in School Communities***. In: Nabors L. (eds) Resilient Children. Springer Series on Child and Family Studies. Springer, Cham https://rdcu.be/cMsYf

***Educators Living in the Joy of Gratitude*** (Free recorded professional development programs facilitated by Kathy Marshall Emerson.)
www.nationalresilienceresource.com/Educator-Preparation.html

***Education and Three Principles*** Christa and Bob Campsall video presentation
www.3pgc.org/photos-videos/details/?m=1185

***Current links to webinars*** with Christa Campsal
www.myguideinside.com

**Selected Principles Publications for Educators**

Aust, B. (2016). Field notes: Capturing the moment with a story. *ASCD Express*. Retrieved from www.ascd.org/ascd-express/vol12/1207-aust.aspx

Aust, B. (2013). *The essential curriculum: 21 ideas for developing a positive and optimistic culture*. Author.

Aust, B., & Vine, W. (2003, October). The power of voice in schools. ASCD *Classroom Leadership*, 7, 5, 8.

Campsall, C. (2005). Increasing student sense of feeling safe: The role of thought and common sense in developing social responsibility. Unpublished master's thesis. Royal Roads University, Victoria, British Columbia, Canada.

Marshall Emerson, K. (2015). "Resilience research and community practice: A view from the bridge." Paper presented to the Pathways to Resilience III, 6/19/2015, Halifax, Nova Scotia.

Marshall, K. (2005, September). Resilience in our schools: Discovering mental health and hope from the inside-out. In D. L. White, M. K. Faber, & B. C. Glenn (Eds.). *Proceedings of Persistently Safe Schools 2005*. 128-140. Washington, DC: Hamilton Fish Institute, The George Washington University for U. S. Department of Justice, Office of Juvenile Justice and Delinquency Prevention.

Marshall, K. (2004). Resilience research and practice: National Resilience Resource Center bridging the gap. In H. C. Waxman, Y. N. Padron and J. Gray (Eds.). *Educational resiliency: student, teacher, and school perspectives*. Pp. 63-84. Greenwich, CT: Information Age Publishing.

Marshall, K. (November, 1998). Reculturing systems with resilience/health realization. *Promoting positive and healthy behaviors in children: Fourteenth annual Rosalynn Carter symposium on mental health Policy*. Atlanta, GA: The Carter Center, pp. 48-58.

**Websites**
   3 Principles Ed Talks: www.myguideinside.com.
   National Resilience Resource Center: www.nationalresilienceresource.com.
   Sydney Banks: www.sydneybanks.org.
   Three Principles Foundation: www.threeprinciplesfoundation.org.

## *Instructional Materials for Pre K – 12 Learners*
myguideinside.com

### *My Guide Inside®* Pre-K -12 Comprehensive Curriculum

Campsall, C. with Marshall Emerson, K. (2018). My Guide Inside, Learner Book I, Charleston, SC: Create Space Independent Publishing Platform.

Campsall, C. with Marshall Emerson, K. (2018). *My Guide Inside, Teacher Manual, Book I*, Charleston, SC: Create Space Independent Publishing Platform.

Campsall, C., Tucker, J. (2016). *My Guide Inside, Learner Book II*, Charleston, SC: Create Space Independent Publishing Platform.

Campsall, C. with Marshall Emerson, K. (2016). *My Guide Inside, Teacher Manual, Book II*, Charleston, SC: Create Space Independent Publishing Platform.

Campsall, C. with Marshall Emerson, K. (2017). *My Guide Inside, Learner Book III*, Charleston, SC: Create Space Independent Publishing Platform.

Campsall, C., with Marshall Emerson, K. (2017). *My Guide Inside, Teacher Manual Book III*, Charleston, SC: Create Space Independent Publishing Platform.

### Picture Book (Pre-K)

Campsall, C., Tucker, J. (2017). *Whooo ... has a Guide Inside?* Charleston, SC: Create Space Independent Publishing Platform.

### Supplemental Books for Parents and Educators

Marshall Emerson, K. (2020). *Parenting With Heart*. Amazon international markets.

Tucker, J. (2020). Insights: *Messages of Hope, Peace and Love*. Amazon international markets.

### Video on Demand Classes and E-books:

Check the website for additional information, updates, and online resources.
myguideinside.com  Password: mgi
Included are Video On Demand classes that bring each chapter to life.

*My Guide Inside® (Book I) Teacher's Manual*

## *MGI in Context of Current Research and Theory*

The *MGI* comprehensive Pre-K-12 curriculum was developed to complement evidence based approaches to effective education and foster student resilience. *MGI* theory stands on the shoulders of significant educational and other relevant researchers such as, but not limited to: Bonnie Benard, Faye Brownlie, Robert Coles, Richard Davidson, Cheryl Dweck, Jenni Donohoo, Michael Fullan, John Hattie, Ann Masten, Parker Palmer, Michael Rutter, Leyton Schnellert, George Villiant, Roger Weissberg, Emmy Werner, Steven and Sybil Wolin.

In every country there are experts dedicated to bringing out the best in students. For example, with leadership of Kathy Marshall Emerson, the National Resilience Resource Center sees every youth as *at promise* rather than as *at risk*.

*MGI* focuses on simple principles operating in all students. Its objectives point to the promise inside every student to: **(1) enhance Personal Well-being, and (2) develop Communication, Thinking, Social Emotional Learning, and Personal and Social Awareness and Responsibility competencies**. These general objectives may be customized to fit specific countries, systems, schools or classrooms.

Authors Barbara Aust and Kathy Marshall Emerson, education and resilience veterans, guided *MGI* conceptual development to clarify the "fit" between *MGI* and established cutting edge global educational efforts and research. These sample resources laying out the "Big Picture" in *MGI* may be especially helpful in discovering this alignment:

- "Personal Awareness and Responsibility Competency Profiles" from British Columbia's Ministry of Education provides the basis for *MGI* learning objectives at https://curriculum.gov.bc.ca/sites/curriculum.gov.bc.ca/files/pdf/PersonalAwarenessResponsibilityCompetencyProfiles.pdf
- "Fitting in with Other Programs" at http://www.nationalresilienceresource.com/Fitting-In.html suggests how principles curriculum like *MGI* complements existing school initiatives and programs.
- "Educators Living in the Joy of Gratitude," facilitated by Kathy Marshall Emerson, includes 12 presentations by veteran educators describing learning, living and sharing the principles in schools globally for the last 40 years. Available from: http://www.nationalresilienceresource.com/Educator-Preparation.html
- *MGI* rests on an essential research base such as "References Relevant to BC's Curriculum Assessment and Transformation" at https://curriculum.gov.bc.ca/sites/curriculum.gov.bc.ca/files/pdf/references.pdf

For a deeper examination of relevant research see the selections that follow.

## ADDITIONAL SCHOLARLY PUBLICATIONS

### Education Research and Theory
Berk, L. (2007). *Development through the lifespan*. Boston: Allyn and Bacon.

Brownlie, F., & Schnellert, L. (2009). *It's all about thinking: Collaborating to support all learners*. Winnipeg, MB: Portage & Main Press.

Cicchetti, D., Rappaport, I., Weissberg, R. (Eds.). (2006). *The promotion of wellness in children and adolescents*. Child Welfare League of America. Washington, D.C.: CWLA Press.

Coles, R. (1990). *The spiritual life of children*. Boston: Houghton Mifflin Company.

Donohoo, J. (2016). Collective efficacy: *How educators' beliefs impact student learning*. Thousand Oaks: Corwin Press.

Dweck, C. (2006). *Mindset: The new psychology of success*. New York, NY: Random House.

Fullan, M. (2016). *Indelible leadership: Always leave them learning*. Thousand Oaks, CA: Corwin Press.

Fullan, M. (2001). *Leading in a culture of change*. San Francisco, Jossey-Bass.

Hattie, J. (2015). The applicability of visible learning to higher education. Scholarship of teaching and learning in psychology, 1(1), 79-91.

Hattie, J. (2011). *Visible learning for teachers: Maximizing impact on learning*. New York, NY: Routledge.

Hattie, J. (2009). *Visible learning: A synthesis of over 800 meta-analyses relating to achievement*. New York, NY: Routledge.

Palmer, P. (1998). *The courage to teach: Exploring the inner landscape of a teacher's life*. San Francisco: Jossey-Bass Publishing.

Reclaiming Youth International. (1990). *Circle of courage*. Retrieved from https://www.starr.org/training/youth/aboutcircleofcourage

Roehlkepartain, E., King, P., Wagener, L., & Benson, P. (Eds.). (2006). *The handbook of spiritual development in childhood and adolescence*. Thousand Oaks, CA: Sage Publications.

Schnellert, L., Widdess, N., & Watson, L. (2015). *It's all about thinking: Creating pathways for all learners in middle years*. Winnipeg, MB: Portage & Main Press.

### Resilience Research and Theory
Benard, B. (2004). *Resiliency: What we have learned*. Oakland, CA: West Ed.

Benard, B. (1991). *Fostering resiliency in kids: Protective factors in the family, school, and community*. Portland, OR: Northwest Regional Educational Laboratory.

Benard, B. & Marshall, K. (1997). A framework for practice: Tapping innate resilience. *Research/Practice*, Minneapolis: University of Minnesota, Center for Applied Research and Educational Improvement, Spring, pp. 9-15.

Davidson, R. J., & Begley, S. (2012). *The emotional life of your brain: How its unique patterns affect the way you think, feel and live – How you can change them*. New York: Hudson Street Press.

Marshall, K. (2004). Resilience research and practice: National Resilience Resource Center bridging the gap. In H. C. Waxman, Y. N. Padron and J. Gray (Eds.). *Educational resiliency: student, teacher, and school perspectives*. Pp. 63-84. Greenwich, CT: Information Age Publishing.

Marshall, K. (November, 1998). Reculturing systems with resilience/health realization. *Promoting positive and healthy behaviors in children: Fourteenth annual Rosalynn Carter symposium on mental health policy.* Atlanta, GA: The Carter Center, pp. 48-58.

Masten, A. (2014). *Ordinary magic: Resilience processes in development.* New York, NY: Guilford Press.

Rutter, M. (1990). Psychosocial resilience and protective mechanisms. In D. Ciccetti, A. Masten, K. Neuchterlein, J. Rolf, & S. Weintraub (Eds.), *Risk and protective factors in the development of psychopathology* (pp.181-214). New York: Cambridge University Press.

Shapiro, S. & Carlson, L. (2009). *The art and science of mindfulness: Integrating mindfulness into psychology and the helping professions.* Washington, DC: American Psychological Association.

Sternberg, E., (2001). *The balance within: The science connecting health and emotions.* New York, NY: W.H. Freeman & Co.

Vaillant, G. (2012). *Triumphs of experience: The men of the Harvard grant study.* Cambridge: The Belknap Press of Harvard University Press.

Werner, E. & Smith, R. (2001). Journeys from childhood to midlife: Overcoming the odds. Ithaca, NY: Cornell University Press.

Werner, E. (2005). What can we learn about resilience from large-scale longitudinal studies? In S. Goldstein & R. Brooks (Eds.), *Handbook of resilience in children* (91-106). New York, NY: Kluwer Academic/Plenum.

Wolin, S.J. & Wolin, S. (1993). *The resilient self: How survivors of troubled families rise above adversity.* New York, NY: Villard Books.

## Three Principles in Education

Aust, B. (2016). Field notes: Capturing the moment with a story. *ASCD Express.* Retrieved from www.ascd.org/ascd-express/vol12/1207-aust.aspx

Aust, B. (2013). *The essential curriculum: 21 ideas for developing a positive and optimistic culture.* Author.

Aust, B., & Vine, W. (2003, October). The power of voice in schools. *ASCD Classroom Leadership*, 7, 5, 8.

Campsall, C. (2005). Increasing student sense of feeling safe: The role of thought and common sense in developing social responsibility. Unpublished master's thesis. Royal Roads University, Victoria, British Columbia, Canada.

Marshall Emerson, K. (2015). "Resilience research and community practice: A view from the bridge." Paper presented to the Pathways to Resilience III, 6/19/2015, Halifax, Nova Scotia.

Marshall K. (2021) Discovering Resilience and Well-being in School Communities. In: Nabors L. (eds) Resilient Children. Springer Series on Child and Family Studies. Springer, Cham. https://doi.org/10.1007/978-3-030-81728-2_5

Marshall, K. (2005, September). Resilience in our schools: Discovering mental health and hope from the inside-out. In D. L. White, M. K. Faber, & B. C. Glenn (Eds.). *Proceedings of Persistently Safe Schools 2005.* 128-140. Washington, DC: Hamilton Fish Institute, The George Washington University for U. S. Department of Justice, Office of Juvenile Justice and Delinquency Prevention.

## Roots of *MGI*

*MGI* is the first principles-based comprehensive school curriculum. The earliest educators to quietly carry the principles into their schools—Barbara Aust and Christa Campsall—began learning from Sydney Banks in 1975 in British Columbia. Jane Tucker, Marika Mayer and Bob Campsall also began to learn from Sydney Banks in the mid-1970's and all have worked in schools directly with students for many years. By 1993 Kathy Marshall Emerson of the National Resilience Resource Center was integrating the principles in two 20-year school community projects in America. By 2016 the *Educators Living in the Joy of Gratitude* global webinar series documented the experiences of veteran Pre-K-12 educators sharing the principles "inside the schoolhouse."

The outcomes of learning, living and then sharing the principles in education complement many efforts to effectively transform education at all levels. There is growing interest in integrating the principles in education globally. To be successful these efforts must be in alignment with applicable, current curriculum standards in any location; in some cases widely accepted research-based papers provide the bests guidance. Most countries have easily accessible guidelines. These are samples:

American Common Core State Standards Initiative. (2017). *About the Standards*. Retrieved from www.corestandards.org.

BC Ministry of Education. (2016). Curriculum. *BC's New Curriculum*. Retrieved from www.curriculum.gov.bc.ca/curriculum-updates.

BC Ministry of Education. (2016). *Personal Awareness and Responsibility Competency Profiles*. Retrieved from https://curriculum.gov.bc.ca/sites/curriculum.gov.bc.ca/files/pdf/PersonalAwarenessResponsibilityCompetencyProfiles.pdf

"Collaborative for Academic, Social, and Emotional Learning (CASEL). (2017)." *Core SEL Competencies*. Retrieved from http://www.casel.org/core-competencies/

"Personal, Social, Health and Economic (PSHE) Education." *Gov.UK*. Retrieved from http://www.gov.uk

"Promoting Fundamental British Values as part of SMSC in Schools" (2014). *Gov.UK*. Retrieved from http://www.gov.uk

"Secondary National Curriculum." 02 Dec. (2014). Gov.UK. Retrieved from http://www.gov.uk

United Kingdom, HM Government. (January, 2017). *Gov.UK*. The Government's Response to the Five Year Forward View for Mental Health. Retrieved from https://www.gov.uk/government/publications/five-year-forward-view-for-mental-health-government-response

United Kingdom, HM Government. (December 2017). Transforming Children and Young People's Mental Health Provision: Provision of a Green Paper. Presented to Parliament by Secretaries of Departments of Health and for Education from
https://www.gov.uk/government/uploads/system/uploads/attachment_data/file/664855/Transforming_children_and_young_people_s_mental_health_provision.pdf

## *Acknowledgments*

Sydney Banks deeply cared about young people. He knew that if we could help our youth, the world would be "a far, far better place." He was an ordinary man who had an experience that profoundly changed him from the inside-out. For the rest of his life, as a speaker and author, he was dedicated to sharing the universal Three Principles he uncovered: Mind, Consciousness and Thought.

As teachers, school administrators and other helping professionals learned these principles, they consistently reported unusually positive results with children, youth and adults in schools, mental health clinics, businesses, jails and community agencies. The principles *MGI* shares focus on individuals discovering their natural inner wisdom and innate mental health. This understanding is now gaining international recognition and respect. We can all be so grateful for the opportunity to explore the principles' profound life-changing message of hope.

Heartfelt thanks go to the team of volunteer dedicated professionals who assisted me in creating *MGI I*: Kathy Marshall Emerson for co-authoring both the Teacher Manual and Learner Book, Tom Tucker for artful production and formatting and Jo Aucoin for creating our special owl graphics. Thanks also goes to Psychiatrist Bill Pettit for his letter expressing his firm belief that pointing young children to their guide inside restores mental health. Administrators Barb Aust, Dr. Marj Hawkins and Lori Smith graciously discuss living from the principles in early childhood programs.

I am especially grateful to author, elementary teacher and principal Barb Aust who over forty years saw the principles bring out the best in students and teachers. She and Kathy reviewed the *MGI* series extensively and provided important links between the principles, curriculum guidelines, and sound research regarding education, resilience, and related fields. Kathy also initially strongly encouraged me to undertake this curriculum.

My husband Bob Campsall contributed insights and encouraged me every step of the way. Our son, Michael, created the accompanying website for *MGI*. Our four grandchildren reviewed the stories and selected the print font and images for *Learner Book I*. For all children, youth and adult reviewers who offered their suggestions and reflections that moved *MGI* along, many, many thanks!

–The Author

*My Guide Inside® (Book I) Teacher's Manual*

# Overview of My Guide Inside Comprehensive Curriculum

### About the Authors

*Christa Campsall (right) has a 40+ year legacy teaching the principles shared in MGI. This has been the foundation of her work as a classroom teacher, learning services teacher in special education and school-based team chair. She has a BEd and DiplSpEd from University of British Columbia, and a MA from Royal Roads University. Along with MGI curriculum development, Christa facilitates professional development for educators in the global community.*

*Kathy Marshall Emerson (left), National Resilience Resource Center founding director, facilitates long-term school community principle–based training and systems change. Her free and globally available recorded webinar series, Educators Living in the Joy of Gratitude, features international veteran educators' outcomes of sharing the principles for as much as forty years in classrooms, school systems, and student services. She has a MA from the University of Southern California and is adjunct faculty at the University of Minnesota.*

---

*My Guide Inside* is a three-part comprehensive Pre-K-12 story-based curriculum covering developmentally appropriate topics in an ongoing process of learning throughout the entire school career. As a teacher, you choose the level of *My Guide Inside* that is just right for your students in your particular school system: *Book I* (introduction, primary), *Book II* (continuation, intermediate) and *Book III* (advanced, secondary). With this comprehensive curriculum, school leaders will be able to chart a continuous instructional plan to share the Three Principles with students as they move through the grades.

**Objectives of** *My Guide Inside (Book I)*: The principles discussed in this learner book operate in all people, including every student. This MGI curriculum points the way to wholeness, happiness, creativity and well-being in all parts of life.
Therefore, MGI has these two globally appropriate academic goals to:
**(1) Enhance Personal Well-being with an understanding of these principles, and**
**(2) Develop competencies in Communication, Thinking, and Personal and Social Awareness and Responsibility.**
*MGI* accomplishes both goals by using stories, discussion and various written and creative activities, as the learning increases your students' competency in English Language Arts and several other areas.

Discovering their guide inside is key to learning, and it enhances children's ability to make decisions, navigate life, and build healthy relationships. Accessing this natural wisdom affects well-being, spiritual wellness, personal and social awareness and responsibility, and positive personal and cultural identity. Social and emotional learning, including self-determination, self-regulation, and self-efficacy, is also a natural outcome of greater awareness of one's own inner wisdom/"guide inside." See what kids think: watch the My Guide Inside Overview (5min) and Focus Group Experiences with My Guide Inside video of secondary student outcomes: 5min summary or full 27min interview myguideinside.com.

The *MGI Teacher's Manual* accompanies *My Guide Inside Learner Book I*. The learner book, under separate title, offers a hopeful, simple way for learners to become aware of how they operate mentally from the inside-out. This understanding maximizes personal well-being and improves school climate, learner behavior and academic performance.

The *MGI Teacher's Manual* contains lesson plans, pre- and post-assessments, activities, evaluation scales and resources. We introduce universal principles making this curriculum for global use with all learners. In addition, we reference curriculum guidelines from Canada, the United Kingdom, and the United States.

- *MGI* meets selected requirements for *English Language Arts, Health Education, Career Education and Personal, Social, Health and Economic Education.*
- *MGI* supports inclusion and develops *Communication, Social and Emotional Learning, Personal Well-being Awareness, Social Responsibility and Thinking* competencies.

*My Guide Inside Book I* is appropriate for all learners in any primary classroom, older learners on a modified program, home learners, self-directed learners working independently, individual learners in counseling or personal coaching and in discussions with parents. Reading Level is "Very Easy to Read." Ideal Participation Level is primary (ages 7-8); adapt for early primary (ages 5-6). A discussion of the early childhood context is included. Most importantly this comprehensive curriculum offers a flexible framework to customize, adapt or modify to fit each teacher's understanding of the principles and the needs of students.

*My Guide Inside*® is available at myguideinside.com
**Check the website for**: E-books, MGI Online for schools, Video On Demand Classes, Online Resources, Translations, Training for Educators, and More…

*My Guide Inside® (Book I) Teacher's Manual*
*What Professionals Say About My Guide Inside*

"I have been a teacher in underserved schools in Baltimore, Miami and the Bronx for over 12 years. By sharing the simple understanding that students are able to decide how they wish to experience life through their choices about thought, I have seen aggressive students become peacemakers, shy, self-conscious children become confident leaders, and the level of consciousness and empathy raised in an entire school. I am thrilled that this curriculum will be seen and experienced by so many! This understanding has the power to change education and the school experience on a global scale!"

*Christina G. Puccio, MEd*
*MGI Video on Demand Discussant, Teacher, Mentor Teacher, PS 536, Bronx, NY, US*

"Words fail my deepest desire to say 'Thank You' for the *My Guide Inside* materials. The knowledge they contain is a gift for every child."

*Dr. Virgil Wood, Educator*
*Author In Love We Still Trust: Lessons we learned from Martin Luther King Jr., and Sr.*
*Houston, TX, US*

"I like the *My Guide Inside* stories that teachers could read and discuss. Consistent vocabulary from K-3 is useful so children can continue to use the knowledge and skills they learn from grade to grade as they move from one teacher to another. It is really wonderful that you put this together. I highly recommend adding your program to schools' zones of regulation for young children."

*Linda Backerman*
*Primary Teacher, Vancouver, BC, CA*

"I am so happy *My Guide Inside* will help many teachers and students find their inner wisdom. Their educational experience and personal lives will be enhanced."

*Helen Neal-Ali*
*MGI Video On Demand Discussant, Facilitator, Author OK Forever: A book of hope*
*Tampa, FL, US*

"I was excited to share the information with the students. I added children's books that helped illustrate a specific learning objective. We would also talk about the principles throughout the day in literature or while working through second grade problems… I liked the activities and art projects."

*Primary Teacher, US*

*My Guide Inside® (Book 1) Teacher's Manual*

"Parents and teachers alike will find this a helpful resource as they work with children and youth to find the wisdom that lies inside each one of them, and to develop strategies for solving problems with the help of their own special guide."

*Kelda Logan, MA*

*Principal, Salt Spring Island, BC, CA* "These authentic stories are simple, yet profound, and have the capacity to lead students to their guide inside."

*Barb Aust, BEd, MEd*
*Principal, Education Consultant*
*Author The Essential Curriculum: 21 ideas for developing a positive and optimistic culture*
*Salt Spring Island, BC, CA*

"*My Guide Inside* brings children and youth into contact with their own wisdom. Christa reminds readers about the power of our thinking and support us to practice 'knowing' through listening. The beautiful tapestry of stories helps readers to 'think and see clearly.' This book is an extraordinary resource…a gift for us all."

*Nia Williams, MA*
*Guidance Counselor, Gulf Islands, BC, CA*

"As a headteacher (principal) for over thirty years, I have often witnessed first-hand the restless struggles many children and youth experience as they begin to feel comfortable in their own skin. Christa's straightforward, simple but profound curriculum helps teachers to point youth in a different direction, to our guide inside, our essence, our wisdom. I would recommend this guide to teachers as a powerful source of support. It helps us all remember who we really are … pure love."

*Peter Anderson, Cert. Edn. Adv. Diploma (Cambridge)*
*Three Principles Facilitator, Headteacher Advisor, Essex, UK*

"As a teacher with many years' experience working with children and teens, including high risk who, for many reasons, did not fare well in the education system, I welcome this inspiring curriculum with great appreciation and respect. At last, here is a different conversation available for schools, one that teaches a simple and straightforward path to securing emotional stability and healthy states of mind. This is the missing piece education so dearly needs."

*Sue Pankiewicz, BA, PGCE*
*Education Consultant, Former Senior Teacher for Special Education Unit, Colchester, UK*

# My Guide Inside® Comprehensive Curriculum

www.myguideinside.com

well-being
communication
responsibility
resilience
social emotional learning
relationships
academic success
self-efficacy
happiness

*My Guide Inside* (MGI)… designed to bring out the best in all students

*Check out the other My Guide Inside Books!*

*Whooo … Has a Guide Inside?*
*(Picture Book) with Pre-K activities*

*Learner Book & Teacher's Manual for:*
*My Guide Inside (Book I) Primary*
*My Guide Inside (Book II) Intermediate*
*My Guide Inside (Book III) Secondary*

*For: Video On Demand Classes, Online Resources,*
*E-books, MGI Online, Translations and More …*
[myguideinside.com](myguideinside.com)

Made in the USA
Columbia, SC
15 May 2024